Kristian Carlsson
Prom of Poems

English books by Kristian Carlsson

Small Press, or Else (Dracopis Press, Sweden, 2013)
One-Hitting the Wonders (Dracopis Press, Sweden, 2016)
A Crack at the Origins (Moria Books, USA, 2016)
Dhaka Poems (Locofo Chaps, USA, 2017)
The United World of War (Locofo Chaps, USA, 2017)
My Melancholy [Audio Book] (Infotunez, Bangladesh, 2017)
A Languishing Chain of Presence; New and Selected Poems 1997-2017, VOL. I
        (Journeyman Books, Bangladesh, 2018)
Covering for Language; New and Selected Poems 1997-2017, VOL. II
        (Journeyman Books, Bangladesh, 2018)
Dhaka Poems [Illustrated Bilingual Edition with Bengal Translation]
        (Journeyman Books, Bangladesh, 2019)
Strophe Signs (Timglaset Editions, Sweden, 2021)

Dracopis_011
Kristian Carlsson: Prom of Poems
ISBN 978-91-87341-18-2

Poems written in English
© Kristian Carlsson, 2023
Printed by Ingram, 2023
Published by Dracopis Press, Sweden, 2023

beard@dracopis.com   www.dracopis.com

Prom of Poems

Kristian Carlsson

Dracopis Press

Prom of Poems

Moebius Strip of Ambition

I ardently find the right word.   *It was expected.*
You adamantly write a line.   *No problem*
I boldly write a verse.   *That's a breach.*
You bravingly write a poem.   *Couldn't care less.*
I creatively write a suite.   *Presentably common.*
You capriciously write a chapbook.   *There's no end to it.*
I disdainfully write a collection.   *Couldn't be more convenient.*
You didactically write an epic.   *Spotted in the distance.*
I exacerbatingly continue writing.   *No abundance.*
You effortlessly continue writing.   *A shining light.*
I fabulously get mentioned.   *Didn't hear it from me.*
You phenomenally get an honorable mention.   *Wouldn't say so.*
I gradually get a short paragraph.   *And trenchant it is.*
You graciously get a full review.   *The rumor goes.*
I high-strungly get a review.   *Read all about it!*
You're honorably reviewed everywhere.   *Except for Nowhere.*
I indistinctly get an invitation.   *Out of the blue.*
You're insistently invited everywhere.   *It gives me the blues.*
I jinglingly get longlisted.   *Seems to be a long list.*
You jangingly get shortlisted.   *Another yawn.*
I kaffeeklatschingly get shortlisted.   *A thorn in anyone's side.*
You kind-spiritedly win.   *Tears me apart.*
I limpingly win.   *I'm on a spell.*
You're lasciviously appointed the next judge.   *Take it easy.*
I magically no longer win.   *Put some effort into it.*
You mindingly win the rest of what there is.   *What's out there, anyway?*
I naively replace you as judge.   *There's much out there still.*

You're neededly appointed judge for the rest of what there is.   *No,*
not much out there after all.

I obviously no longer win.   *As I was saying.*

You ostentatiously no longer need to win.   *Solve your issues.*

I pantingly start to teach.   *Deal with your problems.*

You pityingly write the tutorials.   *They can't write themselves.*

I queerly create new sub-subjects.   *A willingness to improvise.*

You quaintly write new tutorials.   *Is this for real?*

I rudimentarily run the faculty.   *As royalty.*

You're renditionally a consultant to all such faculties.   *No mistake*
about it.

I strayingly renew the classes.   *It's a long story.*

You sternly rebuild new classes.   *Not a compliment.*

I trustingly go back to the old schedule.   *It takes guts.*

You temptingly renew the schedule.   *Another day at the office.*

I understandably rebuild the schedule.   *As if under attack.*

You unyieldingly go finding the right word.   *Can't be lured back.*

I viciously go writing a line.   *Have to wait for it.*

You wrenchingly go writing a verse.   *With a purpose.*

I wittily go writing a poem.   *Holding my breath.*

You x-rayingly anticipate me.   *In a split second.*

I x-file-ishly foresaw that.   *All there is to it.*

You zilchingly miss that.   *Out of pity.*

I zombie-ishly forget all about it.   *That's not even human.*

Continuation as is expected, but neither human.   *It will be worth*
the pain... the pain.

Expansive Poem

There was this theme song I was thinking
could be made for the work,
and then a poem might be put up for franchise.
That's all I can think about, you know.
It could be a happy piece, or not.
I don't think I should make those calls already.
It could scare too many potential franchisers off.
I think I just need to have it meet
all the requirements on a rudimentary level,
in terms of the sentiment and general feel to it—
cut everyone some slack, people do like that,
while still having something to build upon.
Later I'll present something more palpable,
a few characters, partial background stories,
names, of course, names and prospects of eventual
recognition, as they should each in their own way
make you understand how to live life, saving in on lessons
otherwise needed to be learned on the floor,
in all—the package of not too much and not too little;
but to all there is to it,
what is to be had should
be held in fair amounts.
I know you'd like to be in on it from the start,
so let's take the lead as well, while we're ahead,
if we really are, with all the focus on superheroes,
the laurels of those franchises. I'm telling you, this will be
something just as big for us, though proportional to the lesser value

of a new trademark, but big, though proportional to the lesser value
of poetry, but still, biggish, though proportional to the lesser value
of you and I, but still and even more so, we'll franchise the hell
out of that composition, as soon as we know what it could look like
in other peoples' minds, the timing is amazing
for the bigger picture, that's where the promises will be made,
where lies the dreams unstoppable, unless faced by poetry when
reality—could it exist—should've kicked in—
as there lies reality incurable
in the underlying personage.
Dreams unstoppable, for sure,
so how about the underlying personage.
Are you on board?

The Breach of a Poem

Your batterymate—figuratively speaking—
endorsed—metaphorically speaking—
the cockfight—allegorically speaking—
doing business—parallelly speaking—
on the fly—parablely speaking—
but that's not you—literally speaking—
it's the cock in you—anatomically speaking—
bringing out the worst in you—everythingly speaking—
even in spirit—unspiritually speaking—
and in me—poetically speaking—
so he's next—duelingly speaking.

The one who's next—
it's literally not you.

The Bodyguard Clause

In the end, it needed to be omitted—
that condescending excuse of a poem.
I'm not sure why I
got it going in the first place.
Headed three rows down
it didn't look the least memorable,
and it wouldn't let me edit
as little as the punctuation,

and if you allow me to nonetheless
speak on its behalf, I can assure you
it humbly acknowledges and appreciates
your concern and expectations—
if it had been up to the poem,
it naturally would have appeared,

but the poet is somewhat of
a caretaker and a guardian—
if only a dog, if only a child,
but no threat makes a poem shiver.
No magic word can set it straight.

It was as it should be, but didn't suit me the least.
Probably it will turn up from someone else's hand.
That's the nature of a poem, all right,
never leaving us alone. Continually
on the lookout for someone

who'll take the bait.

And I can assure you the rumors are true.
There's a contest going on among the less fortunate poems—
having no chance to ride shotgun and get their names
on the covers, they compete over who gets the most writers
to make an attempt. The kind of manifold interaction
only a movie script can stomach.

They're orphans, really, self taught and all,
and now believing themselves solvent enough
to have people place bets on their game,
apparently imagining we, should we win,
will settle for a handful of random nouns,
a partly worn down case set of Garamond italics,
or a truckload of exclamation points.

Someone better call the Gambling Commission
and put an end to this madness
before any old pair of rhymes get hurt—
get their arms twisted, in over their heads,
thinking the world of a well spent comma,
not having a single cent to their names.

It didn't take long before a bunch
came crawling without even taking
the time to scrape off the names of their
previous originators, not that it bothered them either.
They wore the signatures as memorabilia on their sleeves.

Say I got myself a mercenary poem,
but at least I will get out of my predicament
in one piece and live to not tell about it

even if I have the scars to prove it.

Poems can high-stakedly turn any direction,
drag you down the street—this replacement poem
actually is put in circulation only
to bite the head off of that other poem
should it at long last decide
to search its way back to me in disguise
with sharpened claws of *why*
extended down every baseline.

The Predicament Poem

I know, people loathe hearing complaints
from the wealthy and the poets alike—
I could've earned more on this
if assigned to design the book cover
than by writing it;
I could've earned more if assigned to proofread it;
naturally, I could earn a lot merely resisting from writing it.

And I do refuse to write it, but it practically writes itself.
I refuse to read what is written, but I virtually remember it by heart.
Each day I take all hours off from it, then at night,
I wake up in a cold sweat in urgent need
to remind myself it will be written
in the bylines of sleep no matter what.

The predicament being, people who only ever
excelled in twisting words, corrupting the language—
by whose expertise being lawyer or politician
would be kids' stuff—rarely find anything out there
other than
the advocating for the accumulation of one's own wealth
or becoming a poet.
The lost cases tend to find a job in advertising.

A Broadside with Wi-Fi

Poems aren't that different from people.
As soon as someone does something seemingly wrong,
there's always a poem stepping forward to state what is right.
One time, a skinny broadside poem folded itself into the seat
next to mine. I'm not much of a talker when I travel;
however, I had no choice in my position but to hear it out.
It readily demonstrated its seatbelt buckled under folds
as the inspecting flight attendant passed.
A while later it went berserk;
at first allover my face and then down the isle
as people were trusted not to be
doublechecked when told to keep
electronic devices in flight mode.
It demanded general inspection.
It demanded proof of abidement.
In protest it turned its Wi-Fi back on
streaming poetry readings from the 1980's until
brusquely assisted out of the plane
it started reciting itself with muffled voice
never to be seen again at an airport or any destination.

Conspiracy Poem

I bet, you betcha, it was not meant for me to be invited to this one,
and I bet, you betcha, the reunion will take place online,
and I bet, you betcha, no-one forgot to RSVP,
and I bet, you betcha, even my oldest poems will make an effort to join,
and I bet, you betcha, they at some point will start talking about me,
as I bet, you betcha, they'll realize I'm all they have in common
when done boasting about the size of their languages
and what have become of the words they brought to life.
How about our dear Poet? Has anyone heard any news?
one of them will ask.
And I bet, you betcha, that will get the gossip started, starting in any
direction by one of those I often brought to readings telling its story,
then I bet, you betcha, highly heinous stories will be blurted
by poems that feel I somehow neglected them,
which I bet, you betcha, shall be turned into exclusives by poems that
in change of careers became journalists or influencers,
putting me out there as clickbait
in hope of better assignments and ads,
in hope of more lucrative sponsor deals—
their earnings on the side are their business—
but I bet, you betcha, none of them could've made it as far
without my initial support although most of them I never
heard from again a week after they took their pages and walked.
I bet, you betcha, all of them in some way are helping each other out.
There are those living together in shared housing;
there are those starting schools for the uneducated ones of the others;
there are those making sure the others will get proper funerals;

you see, I know them, and they should undoubtedly find
the decent thing to do if put in seemingly unsolvable situations.

I bet, you betcha, they'll have a good time at the reunion,
and I bet, you betcha, there will be no hard feelings in the end,
and lastly they'll make a promise to do it again next year,
but I bet, you betcha, that won't happen, as when having met this way
the competitiveness begins—leaving each one of them a ruin of its past
though it might take several years for it to come to its fullest extent
and then another few years for them to realize what
has actually happened. Not until then
I bet, you betcha, the next reunion without further ado will
take place and for that one, I'm sure to be seated at their table.
And as this is bound to happen out in the real world,
I bet, you betcha, out of coincidence you'll pass the window and
amazed by such a huge family reunion, feel alone, so alone,
I bet, you betcha, it will break not only your heart
but your whole being into pieces,
and not seeing that happen, knowing I'll find what's left of you
outside as I eventually head home, I will laugh so hard
that the residue of you then will stick to me as to a magnet
and until late that night I'll glue the pieces, but not you, back together,
finally staring at the poem I made out of you, ready to be sent
into the other sphere where I'll have you inflate my other poems.
I bet, you betcha, that was nothing you foresaw happening in your life,
but I bet, you betcha, a great job I will have done with
embedding your double nature, unexposed, as before.
I'm sure you didn't count on me giving you that courtesy.

This Poem Is Not Sponsored

This poem is not sponsored.
What appears in the visualization won't go viral.
Look at this cup of coffee; I will drink it later.
Take a look at me and I'll drink coffee when you're done.
There's nothing in the background. Nothing else in the foreground.
It's understood not to be sponsored. Plain cup, plain content—
I brewed this cup of coffee to re-brand it as a poem and
enjoy it just as well. Take a last look at me with full cup in hand.
When emptied I'll fling it all the way
online—go there to pick shards, will you. This poem can
be licensed to resell under the Copyright Act.
Although the coffee in it will be all the same
luckily it will also taste just the same.
The full cup is already put in my hands by another reader.
A moment later, you once again find shards lying there
that you already found. May this be my bestseller
for you to gather enough shards online
for a million cups, still thinking it's one and the same.
Then you could kind of say you are sponsored,
while my poem still is not; sponsored by Sisyphus, and he'll pay
out of his usual pocket. You really nailed it this time.
I really must admit you really nailed it—
as fast as I could pin it to you.

Leniency

What goes into the poem must come out of the poem.
What we add to the soul must fit into the soul.
What we turn into language must bear to be said.
What is repeated must understand how to grow.
What is ending must have a new path chosen for it.
What goes into the poem must come out of the poem
or have something else come out.
If the soul itself won't fit, settle for a replica.
If a statement might go either way,
settle for silence that might go either way.
If repetition lacks stamina, settle with the replica.
If growth is unending, settle with the continuance.
If the end is terminal, settle with turning around pathless.
But don't hollow the trust poems are forced to put in us.
What comes out of the poem must go into the poem.

Trademarked
by Punctuation

The Period

Presupposedly killing time within context,
well-dressed without a wrinkle,
although not to be called a circle,
dottingly steadfast, ravingly bordersome,
the lowest common denominator
put in writing, wrenched at unconventional
interbindings, once in a while eating
its way through a whole library,
nibbling the bindings unintentionally,
turning the page fingerlessly nimble,
laughing at its own jokes until
two sentences, seemingly simple,
change meaning when thus divided,
as is known periodically will happen,
so the period points out this mishap
pleading to have the copy reprinted,
by wailing each walling sheet down,
no longer a book to safeguard, but who
knows what happens between the sheets
while it happens between the covers

The Comma

Never there as a surprise—
ever ceremonial eradication—
nowhere they astonish—
shafts of oars steadily
rested against baselines—
capital letters the rowers
astray—just an angling
g close by—a waving *a*—
h with arm outstretched
for some wind in the lull—
commas follow protocol
and general command though
acronyms and abbreviations
are scanned for capital endings
where a comma would apply—
to get that galley in motion—
if only a coxswain had given
classes to the lower case
if at least they had seen
a gondola before Gutenberg
changing all praxis off-surged
the letters—no-longer bound
to fine-tunedly billow
by the tremble of a scribe—
waves abating for each line
in print—until suddenly here
—here the commas are—

of digital print—fonts straightened
in unprecedented resolutions—
it's not the wait per se
the commas ponder—
but something is missing—
at least a single ripple
within in all the wait—
yes—there must be
something missing
as far as we do see
that we cannot see

The Colon

Am I interacting
without intervening?
Interlacing a chain of thought?
Bringing both sides
to a common score?

Not as much a team sport
as a team effort?
But can they see the twin star?
Rerouting meaning and context
or just the letters?

A substitute matter
adding its holes to the wall?
An escape route?
The additional supply
for borders to be built?
A pair of peepholes? Portholes?
Do I even need to know?
Rabbit holes? Mouse holes?
If I don't know better than
to act as a colon
on someone else's behalf
does anyone have to know?
If I don't know how to turn around
and look over my shoulder
does anyone need to know?

The Dash

Leaving gaps behind;

allowing for great leaps;

it authentically maps
the mind of the writer;
the mind in the writings;
the mind of the reader;

understood in terms of time;
time spotted on a page
not hard to see as eternal
neither as the fraction
of any instant although there
in front of your eyes
just the same
already or all too soon
enacted out of frame; out of focus;
behind white closed drapes; in spheres
terminally parallel; and right there
the dash; not a figment of imagination
and not a figment for your imagination;
the passer-by
instantaneously
meeting it and having met it
is by implication left with
all and nothing

implied;
implying
nothing at all
to have been explicitly
implied;

what a fidgety figment;
like the Emperor's new clothes
in terms of immanent imagination
it really is a new sight
and nothing of it really seen

The Exclamation Point

Shouldn't have to be misdeemed
as a yell… a howl… a cry…
in fact subtle… the letters are
by arrangement made loud…
that is people talking… hence
subtle indeed… a flagpole
but no flag… an unedged sword…
perhaps it's for the best
to let the exclamation point
take the blame… it can take
the heat… unlike men
sometimes in need
to put two or three
in a row… as if drawing
their execution patrol
and yet another word
is all it takes… no shame
putting all the blame
on this ending of a sentence…
words are hard to come by
and even harder to repeat
with emotional outburst
feathered still… still binding…
emphasized… emphatic or not…

The Question Mark

All too often they are left hanging
as who could do them justice!
Certainly brought to mind
before man could even
speak his mind!
Were brought
into life
to be seen
no question about it!
However everything else
about it is questionable!
They mark the quest for truth
when none is to be had
and uncoyly insist
until we've had
enough and
offer
a bitter lie!
an assisting lie!
an unforgettable lie!
the lie to the best
of one's knowledge!
People taking these lies
swallow them whole
but the question marks won't!
Even the truth when hit on the nail
will be found a perishable piece of Grail!

The Ellipsis

Honestly it feels like a lie:
appearing out of the blue:
not diffidently skipping
but blatantly omitting:
counter-graphically making
a long story short
out of any content
shortened even more
to your discretionary liking
or as the censors want it
or as is left when no-one longer
can remember what or who
the abridgment was supposed
to have had gratified:
or a loss: the worst of losses
unappealing to put words to
in the midst of everything:
most probably invented
to fill up all the gaps
not left behind
by the fault of Sappho
herself
but none the more
a matter of fact:
dot dot dot:
carelessness
negligence

fraternity:
Vive la Répu-dot-dot-dot

The Semicolon

Imagine life without it.
More solid. Statistically static.
Not content with the colon-
part of its name
it would rather paraphrase
"period and comma"
as the Spanish saying goes.
Attributed to colonic fuss
when it clearly causes
none of that sort.
It would be the laughing stock
anywhere figuring in the place
of a colon unless as role-model.
To kill a comma
goes without saying.
The period and the dash.
Even the odd ellipsis.
An empowered glyph.
Just wait until the right bureaucrat
shows up with the original documents
settling its name for all times to come.
No wonder the semicolon sleeps
on a whetstone and gives a whole
new meaning to paper-cuts.
It wouldn't change a thing.
But marriage might.
Whichever kind

of bureaucrat
first comes
knocking
out of brackets
or would that be a parenthesis
out of pondering
it wonders
colonicly
colonially
or however.

Return to the Point of No Exclamation

1

A regressional flax hits the poem with fixed recession—
the coaxed heirloom, into pixels herded

branching itself—out of lexemes—out of letters—in scheme
to reach auxiliary positions, in abundance of de-liaisons

this is to rebuild by preparation
not to compose, neither to write in passing

the poem unravels even the quest for itself
not bringing harm to the… within the… out of the… No,
not at all done being saved into an order out of the ordinary

still me, not at the side of a poem present,
so much into nothing becoming
and in and out of dreams, I no longer find the poem
to give you a rash, like poison ivy, from adjectives in bravery

so prune me, poem, upholstered to the likeness of a poem.

2

The retracted rising—
in the name of the Poet, the Poem
and the Goldy Poetry—hark
a gilded nugget
huffing its puff
a trifle too nimble; rising still
retractedly
toward the Verse, the Paragraph
and the Bloody Sentence—
towering the Word, the Letter
and the Dicky Exclamation Point.
Hark this sparkling Exclamation Point.
Let the examination of it start.

One is bad enough—and two:
each one the void of what
you're unauthorized to say—in full:
capital letter
( )ada, yada, yada
exclamation point times two.
Return to the point of no exclamation.
Portionally plant some
gibberishical jibber-jabber
in between all the gobbledygook.
Now, that's better use of that prattle,
will settle this dabble at puffed drivel.
Let the examination of it rustle.

3

Your language is spying
but you can't seem to find
the traitor in your own self
and continue to think
in words instead of images.
When you consider swearing
your language will certify
the right choice of words
with a new grammar.
When you consider
a love to have had declared
your language tells your mind in writing
to sprawl all obtainable nonsense
across the vocal chords.
You chose letters for high-end phrasings
but your language gives everything away
to poets in instant need of online updates.

Your language is one step ahead of you,
corsage-ing your every step
for the prom of poems
strikingly coming of age,
keeping you one step behind.
Your language unsuspectedly
adds to the notion of your language.
It will tell you when you are ready
to speak in its full sentences.

A comma for your thoughts,
a semicolon for your mind,
a period for your question marks,
an ellipsis for your ellipsis!!

4

We'd better refit your brain somewhat with
Angela Davis, Valery Solanas, Hélène Cixous.
We'll whisk your singular
first-person pronouns
into succus entericus.
We'll put an unpunctuational Earth
behind the acronyms.

We'd better re-brain your fit into some whither whatever.
We'd better brain-fit some of your what-width.
We'll clamp your eyes open—*Clockwork Orange*-style—
with a pair of exclamation points.
We'll hinge together a couple of exclamation points
as a pair of scissors to cut your balls off:

We'll acupuncture your fucking language
with all the punctuation marks of the World.

We'll stuff your cavities with the Armenian kind:

֊

And when you think there's no end to your loss,
we'll throw you this:

؛

And filled with joy, you can hardly believe your eyes—
you shouldn't have—
and believe it to be a semicolon
for your lifeline—O,
pity on your hope—
but it's not—
even if it by likeness appears to be—
this is the Greek kind of question mark,
                        ; is not ;
and we still expect some answers
all the way from Alfa to Omega;
and if they won't come fast enough
we'll have to revive and dart
Bamum question marks at you:

even if it just might kill you—
whereupon we'll just
crack a Vai exclamation point:

and put the pieces over your shut eyes
instead of two coins.

5

The clonal Q&A,
under slippery-when-wet maintenance,
albeit up-and-running
beta stage overturned—
enters like a Fairy Queen
in lieu of any conception of God
to smearingly mimic the meaning of life
unfinished, unleashed,

brand new, out of spare parts,

each question answered
by another question,

rhetorically unbiased by quotation marks
around the question mark.

Mark my words, we're heading for the point of no exclamation;
it's out of our system;
simple math
reaching above our limited field of envisioning
fowlily entr'acting horizons.

There Can't Be Any
End to a Poem

For Gertrude Stein
la miglior fabbra

A

Not to inconspicuously waste
the purgatorial off-season
freewheelingly afterlife-ish
undead-span,
out of convenience seen
in swearword-riddled rage
heading for a new name—
it
the it of it set
it
unfeathered
hinges its wings
beneath language
flapping inside of your expression
to strain the vowels
from all keywords
and have you growl m(e)rc(y)
have m(e)rc(y) on m(y) p(o)(e)m:
Mmrrrcchavemmrrrcconmmmppmmm!!
It's literally not
you
it's
it
in passage
becoming you
having you become
it.

The hauntee no more than the haunted—
merely freaked
out of mind
wouldn't do.
Possessee—
banished autopilot
rebooted dispatch central—
possesse, possesse!!

B

Twitches and even more twitches
trying the electrical switches
bypassing
backtraceable body language
chocking the skin into chirps
muffled jug-jug chirps
as if out of an egg.

Obsolete cracklings—
try retinal switchboard—
head for the electro-chemical
control tower—
hit the lookalike glare—
puppeteer, puppeteer,
puppeteering eyes.

To haunt is to haunt.
To parasite is to intrude.
A symbiosis is symbolic.
The surreal skews static facts.
What has taken place here
is a new reality.
And whenever reality begins
no one knows it has started over.

Neuroplasticity—
you can do nothing but take it from the top.

Whatever becomes a starting point
is bound to be forgotten,
as reality itself
is bound to be forgotten.

C

Recent and relevant
rest and recuperation:
twice the amount of sweet dreams.
Mistletoe in hammerlock.
Waterlocked landfill.
Lockstitched franchise.
Picklocked eyeballs.

Hindsight displacement,

cameo forerunners
add a new moment

for literature to take place.

A rebuked language
now grieves.
Pestering insignias!!

D

You.
Say no more; it's communicated.
You.
It takes you personally to start a fight, says your
language.
You, your language, how many are you in there?
Someone just ruined another draft.
You?
Limit yourself.
Still, the difference
shouldn't be noticeable.

E

Body memory
unendowed with repeal
although the Past changes
faster than the Future.

Ambitions amend
in the cortex.
Before reactions are inaugurated
the completion passes
like the daydream of an infant.

The brain
once again unabridged—
there's no it to it,
the it of it is un-therely there,
it—no-longer what,
it—whatever not prolonged by distance.
The unabridged brain
as if merely changed

from hardcover to pocket,
from one publisher to another,
from hard copy to e-book,
but the new font can't seem to fit the pages,

unabridged—but the punctuation marks are gone,
unabridged—if you say so,

unabridged—if you believe it to be,
unabridged—if the copy is allowed to
                alternately correct the original,
unabridged—with its original lost.

Thus unabridged—this wakes up
saying "it" suddenly forgetting
something was said.

F

Heading for the Z
apparently seems
obvious to all of us.
Following protocol.
Doing it by the book.
Honoring the rules.
This is based on a true story.
To you.
To us it's a rerun. Didn't we tell you?
We're sorry, but we need to cut you short here—
here, anywhere, and everywhere.
From here on, you're on your own
like the rest of yourself.

The conversation is still running.
You couldn't just give all hope up, could you?
Hoping to reckon with protocol.
You do believe in the sanctity of the alphabet—
nothing to be ashamed of—
make some fucking p o e t r i e s ! !

Livestock Alphabet

(1)
Save your words to waste them.
Raise your hands below them.
Blow them into position.
Mark your lines prosaically.
Post yourself there tangibly
waiting.
Deal yourself punctuation marks—
have them blow your deal
with the words.

Arouse your exclamation points
and praise your question marks
to lead them astray.
Let other punctuations dawn
at the baselines—
shield yourself from linear sunburn
with arbitrary lower case letters;

await the upper case demanding grammatic justice
before using your thumb nail to slice
all the periods like pizzas
up for breezy grabs,

sparsely strain all edges of the dashes
to have them staple the flip side
of your sheet to the desk,

shave the profiled mustaches off of the semicolons
before you carefully remove the true commas and
let the all-new goatee-shaven commas drain
pinched to their lines with clothespins made
from pairing the last few exclamation points
in sight somewhere in the margins

before calling it a night
bring your sharpest set
of WWW
offline in order to saw your colons in halves
use the upper parts as periods until further notice
flip the lower ones over and row them up
as coasters at the line breaks
on which to put a U each with warm milk
for the better shards
to make it alluring go for the camel milk

on this night be sure to use
two T:s as earplugs
use a Z to hinge two X:s as an eye mask
use a P to meticulously pick your teeth

and drink no more than one leveled Y of sapless soap
if it won't make you cough up bubbles soon
you've chosen too small a Y
but don't overcompensate
just take a shot from your V as well

then face up flat on the ground you should
put your N and your M within reach
on each side of you in the same fashion
as leg holders on a gynecology chair

but to be used for your arms bent over your head
having everything prepared for the night
to get the picture kindly imagine
your brain as the vagina

depending on your heftiness you should
press either a face-down K
or a standing H over your neck
and weigh it down with your Q

gently fit your D into your mouth
not to accidentally bite your tongue
push a C into your nostrils
to facilitate your breath
have your O at hand as bedpan
just lie still until you fall asleep
and sleep until you wake up by yourself

well
good morning to you
then
get yourself out of your position
and rid yourself of all used equipment

you will need your B as a pair of glasses
and to comb your hair with the E as
if all is as suspectedly expected and
a single question mark has sneaked
its way back and thus will fall from its
comforting hiding place in your hair
just screw it thoroughly into the wall
as a hook in front of your desk
to hang your A on at eye level

with your F as caliper
you now will measure
the paper weight of your sheet
and accordingly
as the distanced arms of your F
constitutes the ideal thickness
it should slide in to fit like a glove
if not
your new periods must've spilled
too much milk while drinking
or drunken too little of it and hence
not drooling enough while doing it
so that liquids either way
weren't soaked up evenly
though
if you did use camel milk
such issues are unprecedentedly unlikely
if for some reason however
any inconsistency occurred
you should use your J to scoop and your L to scrape
redistributing the coat of drooly milk until
necessary results are measurably achieved

mind you
if you can't seem to ever get past this stage
you'll only have four letters to your name
and the fact that they spell GRIS might not
alarm you all that much
but be reminded it's the Swedish word for 'pig'
just succeed satisfactorily

and now there's no turning back
but if you've been too greedy with the font size

you might need to brace yourself
as you have to thrust that blunt I of yours
deep enough into your thumb
to draw a drop of blood big enough
within the single first drop only
to fill the hollow of the R all the way
down its bowely abyss

lastly wedge your S into the G and pull
as if pulling your mother's heart out
until the neck of the G caves
and it closes clammed as an O

and from this non-O O
your new alphabet will perkily spring

but first you need to assemble
your semi-new commas
and your semi-new periods
into new semicolons to be attached
as pointy claws on your fingers
and used for giving this O
an all around caressing tickle
gently until it cracks
by its inner self
like an egg

leaving the shell as a parenthesis
releasing the reincarnations of all your letters

and as if afterbirthly descending a uterus
from each half of the parenthesisly parted shell
with reversed gravity

your rejuvenated punctuation marks
follow like a dual placenta

and from now on all your prose
will turn into highly graduated poetry

this is your character set
use no other letters in your life
treat them as a samurai would his sword
as an artisan baker would his sourdough
as you would the skull for your hamlet-
impersonation if you weren't here

do feel free to grab your Capital Letters now
and put them to Good Use Again
and while your at it
pull a period out of that placenta
as I forgot my spare ones at home
My daughter is in a monochrome
phase and used them all up
on a bead pegboard
I need one of yours now
—welcome to the real world—
to bring these instructions
to an end
But not to degradedly offend
any unique notions
of your proper alphabet
and punctuations
I'll honor the loan as a quote:
' '
.

(2)
Now—in terms of maintenance:
make sure to clean
their private parts regularly;
especially the K and Z
makes it a challenge;
the H should always wear diapers
when not on display;
have the Q circumcised and sterilized
as soon as you get home;
in wintertime put a sock on the L;
what else, yes, don't treat them as pets,
they can't be trained for nothing;

the E doesn't appreciate
being rushed into essay;
make sure no kids will get hold of your F
and pretend it is a machine gun
as it might coincidentally
have loaded itself with periods
and someone will get shot;

in terms of safety, always keep the S and the X
divided by another letter, not to blow a fuse;
and don't let T get into a fight with the A,
as T is likely to dropkick the hell out of it;
if the G gets an unreachable rash
on the inside of its stress
just throw a comma
into its open counter
and shake it like hell
five minutes or so;

you should limit the screen time
for your W
more so than for a child;
now and then the V might sneak out to party,
and to not have it indisposed the following day,
you might want to allow it to use the J
pivoted as a crotchy cane;
although the D always looks pregnant,
at times it might actually be pregnant,
but respect its privacy;

occasionally you should allow the M, the Y, and the I
some time off to practice their cheerleading pyramid positions
not to foolhardily strain an ankle or two when at the OLYMPICS;
don't let the R naggingly fool you into buying a dog;
if you're into compact living and every dot counts,
you might want to consider
making the O more balloony
and squeeze it into the U,
but don't try anything similar
with one of the other letters;

people have been reported to go crazy for real from a prank
popular in the P community—if your P appears to be
too saintly, almost a saint, first precautionarily check
if it has put your C skewedly on its head;
and if you can't find your N, having looked everywhere,
and turned everything upside-down, most likely
it's pulling your nose, having flipped over into a Z;
and with the B you should obtain a love-hate relationship,
to prevent, prohibit and detain it from discovering
that it is actually a species of butterfly,
and in case of emergency with such emergence,

and the wings are already spread, you should
at all times have four periods readily available
in your pocket, to weigh it down,

although I happen to have none of that sort today,
and quotably beg of you another finalizing
'.'

(3)
And furthermore it's advisable
to pick neutralizing nicknames
for each and every one of them,
punctuation marks included,
not to get your friends and relatives,
all acquaintances and potential bystanders,
confused when
talking about your day you just
need to spill your guts out;

you don't want to be caught saying,
I couldn't hold my P today,
I got screwed by my X again,
my H is playing me over,
I couldn't care less about R-U-O-K,
I dropped my Q,
I swear I will kill J one of these days,
if only I wasn't this drawn to B-S,
oh G, it's clear Y-I hate thee now,
T makes me puke,
what was Z to me, anyway,
as far as I can see there's nothing special to C,

I have to share my suspicions about the W with you,
you know, it feels like I'm being spied on,
can I stash my E at your place, I don't think it's safe
to leave it at home while I'm away,
all night I had D stuck in the colon,
I would like to tell the world about my amazing period,
it's all eyes on the parenthesis nowadays,
I need to leave more space for N-V,
caught between the sheets, M-L got separated,
I'm literally in a co-comma-comatose state,
F-A gave me disturbing news—
well, you get my drift'.'

(4)
That would be all for now
if it hadn't been for the need to directly address
your scruples—and reprimand them into
cautious awarenesses of prevailing politics
in the poetry society'.'

Your livestock alphabet
is a privilege that will grate on poets
and to avoid having one of them
shakespearingly pull a dagger on you
for appearing between the same covers,
anthologized, or what else,
it's of immanent importance
that you
never share any kind of poem in any sort of way
without having made sure it is harmless, safely
sealed by quotation marks

or enclosed in brackets'.'
It will look ridiculous, but in the end
it shall turn out to be a lifesaver—
in case your letters
haven't gotten the best of you by then
and pulled you into their madness
of non-primate behavior
instead of the other way around, just because
you yourself, immediately starstruck,
allowed it to get that far'.'
Stop looking at the letters now
to get them out of the whole picture
and treat them all the same one-on-one
although it's practically impossible'.'
To keep your character set alive
this is the impossible thing
you are expected to do'.'
Put love and hate aside,
poetry is about language,
and it takes living letters, like yours,
to change language into
either of the languages
the language will become'.'

And speaking of chosen ones
from now on we should only
communicate through lawyers
and to get our healthy enmity going
I will soon end with an 'unquoted' period
that I urge you to bill me for
and for which I tenaciously contradictive
will drag you to court—
welcome to reality,

bring everything you have into it,
you'd need it to make yourself needed
as badly as I need a cup of coffee,
as if there was time for any of that,
the bringing or the brewing,
when people stand in line
for crossable language
to zigzaggingly come to terms
with having minds of the human format,
caring for nonsense
as a historian would for scattered remnants,
as a bird would for feathers,
as a dragon would for mythology-inclusiveness,
as a letter would for its nearest neighbors in the alphabet
as a letter would for its nearest neighbors in a word,
care
as I care for nonsense,
ready to save it
at the cost of language.

(5)
As bad as I need the coffee,
coffee built the body of this informative poem
and thus shaped it as an autoscopy experience
for my livestock alphabet—
as you might gather
coffee is our biggest fan,
the ever-present connoisseur
spotting each and every page of ours,
pun intended,
and according to the Ode to Coffee,

which I now interpretament-intendedly more or less quote,
a coffeedly composed poem
can only be understood by a coffee-eyed critic,
and that, and all the aforementioned,
is all there is to it,
although some people say you should just go ahead and write,
as if writing has all that much to do with poetry
when poetry is all about languaging language in between
punctuations and line brakes—
until someone tells you to go to bed,
most often it tends to be
your mother calling to say goodnight at her own bedtime,
mine still lecturing me about staying up longer than her,
although I'm in my forties now, and have a family of my own,

and that's an excuse as good as any
to put a sudden end to a poem,
just imagine
—on so many levels—
the tunnel-visioned unendingness
—on so many levels—
right in front of you,
if it hadn't been
—on so many levels—
for my mother,
when, per definition, there can't be any end to a poem,
such factual endings are presupposedly implied
only for things predominately getting written,
as in just go ahead and write, but
like language, poetry just s e e m s t o

Less Than Poetry
Was Expected of Life

Hades Second-Guessed in Reverse

I have written poems bound for sure to die young.
To keep this piece on foot, I have removed the wings:

Into Achilles skiddedly built each single verse:
the weak-link heel—by frolicking whims
unlicked—will override immortality's plight.

       Poem submerged,
       no heads up
       to heel twistedly hid
       as a top-to-toe
       versatility heeds
       eternity to the brim.

Now, Reader, I ask of you to kill your darlings in here:
Reel this poem in afloat; deduce its darting body.

Onto Icarus wideningly brim each stifled line:
before waxen flames—the wavered dreams
unwallowing—reheated by the reader's might.

       Find that heel
       to shape your wings.
       But until then It
       may walk on water.
       No, let that water
       walk as It.

No Life-Changer

Lewd truths and serious jokes.
A little out of sorts
if you were in my position.
It must also be okay to tell the truth,
to bear to hear the truths that can't
be believed more than lies.
It's normal, or could be,
tend to maybe be possible to be.
I'm sorry about everything.
You shouldn't have to think this much.
You have assets.
You have pets.
You have a dentist's appointment.
You have no lewd truths.
You know no serious jokes.
To tell you the truth, and I shouldn't, as this isn't
one of the lewd ones, you're doing the right thing.
Save your time.
Now we're talking.
Fake news, whatever.
What's streaming next?

Poem Surrounded by Stones

In terms of safety
my poems should be considered stones.

Only kids throw stones at a fool;
grown ups throw stones at the threat
pulling the carpet from under their feet.

It's foolish to become a poet,
but poets are no fools.
Fools throw stones
at stones.

Not Quite a Bird Poem

1

I read somewhere it's men who
most commonly tend to write about
birds. The species can be accounted for.
We all know which one is most popular.
Particular birds in poems are never trending.
Am I expected to add a bird to this now?
That might be offensive to my style.
I'll just settle for an egg then:
outsourced as any bird.
The egg in a nutshell.
A feather by proxy.
A beckoning
beak, even.

2

And languishingly came
hearse cloth-language,
vowels vowed with dashes,
fret-away syntax-unleavenedness,
spandexish dexterity,
stipulating nouns,
fanfares, fanfares, fanfares,
hark—the egg.

3

Oval office,
        oval poem,
                oval uterus.   Oval pop song,
                                    oval media,
                              oval critique.
Oval patriarchate,
        oval fatherhood,
                oval son-in-law.   Oval oblivion,
                              oval assumption,
                          oval regret.
Oval greed,
        oval excess,
                oval doom.   Oval brain,
                                oval mind,
                          oval math.
Oval egg,
        bipolar egg,
                tripod egg.

Serial Killer Poem Included

1

I couldn't refrain from
reading bestsellers
as a retractable bucket list
in my youth.

It created in me a sense of
responsibility.
Each time reattaching a piece
of my own personality
to the true story behind
my faulty ambitions.

This portion—constituted in my mind—
a while ago unanimously deducted:
I am striving for conclusion
in a hasty manner, not appropriate for the masses.

I want my pieces to expectedly return
from that portion of my mind—
but never mind the responsibility it raised.
A serial killer could abruptly aim for the masses,
and people take interest in it
in a different fashion than in a mass-murderer.
I could write you a poem about serial killers, if I wanted to;
that's not the issue, the issue being:

I wasn't this angry when I was young, it came with
the enlightenment beyond acceptance
from reading too many bestsellers.

2

There was this guy, you know, and he killed a person,
there was a lot of blunt force trauma going around,
you know, as this guy wanted to become famous,
what was he called, I can't seem to remember,
well, you can check it yourself in one of the biographies,
I think he even wrote his memoirs, and he for one
most certainly would get his own nickname right.
Anyway, he then killed another, then another, then another,
and another few right before his last few.
One would think he could continue like this forever,
but you can't be famous, personality-wise, unless you get caught,
oh, I forgot, there were actually a few others killed as well, along the way,
and who would have ever known that for sure, if this guy, this
elaborate guy wouldn't have stepped forward, pointing fingers
at himself, making a point of himself being the only one able
to point out the locations of the poor bastards who since long
already had their rest in peace, I swear on my life, they did.
And then one day this other guy comes along,
and says, he does, he would like to add some pictures to his book,
that is, he says, he does, that bringing the truth out there
would be benefited by some pictures of the gore,
and that's fine, he is told, and told to wait while
appropriate fees are being calculated in the offices
of who knows—someone who happen to know the one who knows
who took those pictures on site—but, by all means, that's

another story, the pictures will find their way into the book
some way, other ones being saved for a second edition with
even gorier details. But what was all of this good for, again,
let me see, there was a guy, that's for sure,
and he started off killing a person,
and then another, and then another, and then another,
and then another, and then another, and then another…
Maybe it wasn't so much that he killed them,
who knows if they had any commemorative traits, anyhow,
not that I'm saying they didn't, but you better check one of
the biographies to make sure either way, if you care for it,
the biographies of the killer, that is, just so you don't go thinking
you would easily find a book about one of the victims,
all the same, I lost track again, this guy, killing and killing and killing,
he wasn't like the other ones, you know, he wasn't like those guys
hastily concluding peoples' lives—killing, yes,
killing, I mean—so we ought to look into, no torturer either,
what blunt force traumas he caused, killing them, killing them.

3

Now don't you come suing me
for degrading those… those… those…
bestsellers.
They're the best, really,
as best as they come.
Couldn't have been better
sold.
They're so sellable, aren't they?
I would say they are, they most
definitely are, couldn't be better.
Well, maybe a few copies more
could've nailed this one better
in terms of selling best,
compared to bestsellers
that practically sell themselves,
but on the whole, it's a good effort
and still a praisable bestseller—
and boy, it sold, it did sell,
I practically saw it sell myself.
I dare say everybody saw it being sold,
they would have been blind not to see it sell,
that is, if they weren't too busy looking at the ones
that sold more, or at least slightly more—for sure, looking
only at books selling way more than average.
And, you know, it felt really good to handle the sales as well,

it's not always it does, but in this case the feeling of being selling
couldn't be better, it might even be true
that a bestseller with a nicer feel to its sale
never could venture to show up;
even if it never came to be the bestseller
selling best in the whole wide world,
or even, in select parts of the world—
I can't figure out how a better sale,
compared to the feeling of selling the other ones,
would actually come about.
We're not happy with the sales,
don't let anyone think I was saying that,
one's not allowed to ever be satisfied
with any kind of sales figures
when it comes to a bestseller.
I mean, you can't be allowed
to fathom that there might be an end to it.
Don't say that I said that. It's a trade secret.
Only a few carefully selected accountants
and even fewer publishing house directors
and just a handful of book seller CEOs in the world
know the actual calculated truth
about how far any given bestseller might
be capacitated to ever go
in the next four score and seven years.

Cherry Spot Man

Oh: you don't know what I look like, apart from my birthmark.
Sorry. I am small, with a ringletty mass of leonine curls, and in
fact a rather leonine face; I would look good in whiskers.
— From *Little Liar* by Julia Gray

The performance as a matter of digestion of context,
there was no use in entering before having cake,
the Twin Peaks cherry pie will add to your performance face,
the other you, making confessions in spotlight blindness,
putting the you of you on display,
pulling the me in I into our non-discretionary flesh.
How should I possibly have known birthmarks amass?
All the talk of gray hairs to come, but nothing about the
dalmatianisation of man.
It all started with a few cherry spots, cute on a teen,
turning forty these petite red buttons cover my body
like a moth-eaten haute couture swim suit from the 1930's.
Only in Japan my cherry spots are ideal,
a full body tattoo of natural origin, ongoing, unending;
I don't mind the freak show, I'm a legend—
set the rest of me on fire, and keep
the cherry spots in a sacred bowl, will you,
it's the performance of a lifetime—
I do it every year under the falling blossoms
of a Tokyo City cherry tree. Last year
they made me into a solo adventure gamebook:
to set him on fire go to page six,

to set him on fire go to page twenty seven,
to set him on fire go to page ninety nine,
to set him on fire flip to next page.
The kind of superhero Cherry Spot Man is:
saving late spring and late summer,
setting the aftermath of other months on fire.
Had I only been thirty years younger,
my mother would definitely have sown
me the proper costume,
like she probably did sew
the red and black Michael Jackson outfit
with glove and all,
like she probably did sew
the red, white and yellow Salt 'n Pepa outfit
with patches and all.
No real idol comes without a superhero-heroic set of costumes;
sometimes one grows on you, making you instead of marking you;
suddenly changing your pitch as well,
like a second breaking of the voice,
as Darth Vader would understand, as Batman would understand,
the third voice of one's life, if not a flute
a fluent flare, only giving in, lastly,
for the crumbling voice of old age.
Cherry Spot Man has the voice of one
spitting pits in between vowels.
Cherry Spot Man, not unlike the Rat-Catcher of Hamelin,
bringing the flight of insects into a pitfall
towards the nectar of cherry trees.

"That's not particularly heroic, man,"
a villain shouts. Well, let me tell you,
it's a local phenomenon, and during limited time frames,
but more importantly, the rest of the year

I'm at service as the world's only authorized
dry cleaner of superhero suits and attributes.
For me to become Cherry Spot Man
forever,
go to the unpaginated pages
and never return to reality.
Cherry Spot Man, the second coming;
you will see his stigmata
retrogradely burst into full bloom—
go to page twelve to hear him say:
"I would look good in whiskers."

Mowgli Media Span Spam

Unfaithed
mowgliesque man-cub's
bloomed fire-might

Wait!
What's your take on what Mowgli
would say if he could give
—his opinion on *Gremlins*?
—his opinion on *Rambo*?

Mowgli isn't alone as man-cub to
baptize himself in fire as flowering highness

And what would he write about
were he an Influencer or just an everyday Blogger?

I'm in on it with Mowgli
as man-cub to overstep
unfrail-demasked
arc-faces

Fine! But would he stand a duel with Tarzan?
Imagine him in a reality show, any reality show!

The paradigms brought from Mowgli as such would—

Would you say he is a badass bowler? I bet he is! Makes everybody want to plan for further strikes!

Lit de Parades

Mind—on your deathbed I'd rather be one poem short
while imagination vacates.

Body—on my deathbed I better be one poem short
while getting forgotten.

Eternity—on your deathbed, well,
unendingly dying while being immortal,
I couldn't care less.

That one poem short—on its deathbed,
people might as well turn to prose.

Benignifying

The white of the eyes
partitionally recongeal,
uninhibited soothy drool
forked by the tongue
tinges the beard
and laboriously frets a bald furrow
on each side of the mouth,

the fingers stiffen
as the arcs
of the so-called fingerprints—
oscillatingly loosened and tightened
in their drawn paths—
readjust all directional conformity
from the past,

in turns the body rejects counter-intentions
a fraction of a second at the time,
giving the body a detained limp
pacing staccato-like against
the wall-to-wall bookcase
until all books are
piling under unflagging feet,
the dawning times
and a new day
benign.